Beyond the Dash

Preserving Your Family Legacy

Keep the Dash Alive - Facebook Fan Page:

http://tiny.cc/KTDAFB

Keep the Dash Alive - YouTube Channel:

http://tiny.cc/KTDA

Family History Book Template:

http://tiny.cc/fhbtemplate

DEDICATION

As a junior in high school, our US history teacher asked us to put together a genealogical chart going back at least three generations (if possible). I had never heard of family history research until this project was given to me, and I was amazed at how much my family knew about its past.

My parents and grandparents knew quite a bit and it was very easy for me to put this project together for class. I was fascinated by some of the names and the migration pattern. From that point I was hooked on preserving family history and stories.

I worked on the family history for quite a while and then my parents got involved in their retirement. This book is dedicated to my parents, Cecil Lewis Bonner and Mary Belle Skelton Bonner, both of whom passed from this earth in 2014. This book is a tribute to them and their passion for our family histories.

In addition, this book is a legacy for my niece and nephew, Michaela Bonner and Jonathan Bonner. This book will help them to pick up where my generation leaves off, if they choose to, or if they find they have an interest in the subject area. I have written this book with Michaela and Jonathan in mind, or my future generations of nieces and nephews that I may never meet. Whichever niece or nephew picks this up in the future, I am here to help you to have an idea of what to do with the rich history you come from, as well as the rich history you will write after me.

Finally, my hope is that this book inspires future generations of family researchers beyond my family unit. You will find through the examples in the book that researching and documenting your family history is an enriching and fascinating process. Fellow historians, your past, present and future awaits, let us begin!

FAMILY HISTORY BOOKS

Of Good Disposition – Bonner Family, Soft cover: http://bit.ly/bonner-s

Of Good Disposition – Bonner Family, Kindle Version: http://bit.ly/bonnerk

Writers, Fighters and Poets – Harper and Cagle Families of Alabama, Kindle Version: http://bit.ly/harper-k

Writers, Fighters and Poets – Harper and Cagle Families of Alabama, Soft Cover: http://bit.ly/harper-sc

Elmore, Brown, Sharpton and Strickland: Families of Pickens County, Alabama, Kindle Version: http://bit.ly/elmore-k

Elmore, Brown, Sharpton and Strickland: Families of Pickens County, Alabama, Soft Cover: http://bit.ly/elmore-s

Skelton, Albritton and McGee Families: Soft Cover: http://bit.ly/skelton-s

Skelton, Albritton and McGee Families: Kindle Version: http://bit.ly/skelton-k

DISCLAIMER

This book is written at a point in time. My goal is to not go into a lot of technical detail about any of the technology tools, i.e., Microsoft Word, Snag It, or Ancestry.com, etc. I will at times show pictures of what I am describing, but just note that new versions of software and websites happen on a frequent basis. Thus, if I get too involved with describing exactly where something is located on a menu, the information could become obsolete in less than a year. Therefore, I will give you the conceptual framework, so that as technologies change, you have a platform you can operate from no matter what changes or what new tools are introduced. The goal of this book is focused on how to think about being a family historian, what to think about when organizing your historical artifacts, and how to think about putting it all together for publishing a book.

I do have a support YouTube channel (http://tiny.cc/KTDA) – that will provide video support on how to use book templates, how to publish a book very cheaply on Amazon, and how to produce a family history YouTube channel of your own, if you decide you want to use that medium.

In addition, this book is written largely regarding United States resources. The process is similar in other countries – however, I would not be sure if a concept of a "courthouse" is necessarily the same thing in another country. Overall, this book will give a roadmap overview to family history research, but the details per country may be different depending on your location.

PREFACE

2014 began with the news that my father had fallen in the bathroom and hit is head so hard that it caused a brain bleed. He had been challenged with strokes since 2010 and when I learned that he had refused any surgery to try and repair the brain bleed, I knew the end was near.

After a conversation with mom about whether she thought he would lose the ability to recognize me or talk to me, we decided it would be good to make a visit. As we visited with dad, for what would be the final time, my mother and I would discuss family history. It is a project we had been involved with since I was 17 years old. Based on those conversations, we found ourselves in the Arbor Springs Baptist Church cemetery where many generations of Bonners are buried.

At one point mom pointed to one of the headstones and she said, "see, life happens in the dash". For some reason, that one off handed comment got me to thinking.

As we headed into May, 2014, my father passed away on May 12, 2014. At his memorial, I had been thinking about what I wanted to say about him. After all of the funny stories were told, I wanted everyone to know his life mattered. It was my goal to make sure that he lived on after his death.

What do I mean by that? In most family history books that are written, you will find the vast majority of these books to be somewhat sanitary and whitewashed. There are often a bunch of dates and names, perhaps information about marriage dates, maybe even some pictures. But there can often be very little information about stories, writings, or anecdotes about a person's life. Sometimes you may find a letter or two, or a newspaper article, but those can be rare. Sometimes, the sterility is due to people not wanting to publish sensitive information, but by the time the generation has passed, no one has kept the information in order for the story to be told.

It is one thing see "Cecil Lewis Bonner, born April 29, 1937 – died May 12, 2014". It is a completely different experience to see this in addition to that: "My mother told me that he was a hands on father when his children were born. He did not have any issues with changing diapers and in fact enjoyed doing that task". It is great to have the statistical detail, but it is another experience entirely to have the rich insight into a person; what they represent, how they thought and felt, and what they stood for in life.

Ultimately, we lost mom in 2014 as well. Her passing was a completely unexpected event on September 28, 2014 due to a complication of a surgery. As much as I write this for future generations, I also write this as a tribute to my parents. They helped me so much to bring to life our family histories, and in keeping my parents alive and vibrant, hopefully future generations of Bonners, Harpers, Elmores, and Skeltons and related families will be inspired to preserve their lives and not be just be a statistical reference. Life is in that dash and the goal is to capture what that dash means for each individual.

Table of Contents

CHAPTER 1: GATHER YOUR DATA

Much has changed from when I started working on my family research in 1980. It is humbling to note that personal computers were not used much in 1980, so gathering family history information required leaving my house and driving to libraries, courthouses, and various other places to find information and hunt down information. My family has walked and driven many a mile to gather information, take pictures, etc.

Even with the advent of more powerful and flexible technology to use, do not forget, sometimes you will have to resort to the old methods. Thus we will start with some basic information about how to do the tried and true walking and driving methods, and we will explore some of the more advanced tools of today.

Future generations will have even more flexible technology tools in the future. The goal of this book is to ground you in fundamental thinking and awareness – awareness is really the key thing here – so that no matter what tools come along, you can embrace those new tools and be aware of how to use those perhaps in unique ways to aid enhancing your family story.

Sources Closest to You

The primary sources of information will be your family. When I started, it was because I was doing a US history project in high school. We were asked to write down our names, birth date, our parents' names, birth dates, and then go three generations back, if we could.

At that time, I knew myself and my parents and three of my grandparents were alive, plus, I had known my deceased grandfather up until the eighth grade – the year he had passed away. I just was not sure everyone's birthdate or where they were born. Beyond that generation I only knew one great-grandparent, Mary Lou (Brown)

Elmore because she passed away in 1981 at the vintage age of 98!

When I told my parents about this project, we got busy writing down what we knew and then we went to see my grandparents. They started filling me in on names of people I had never heard of, names that were really unusual, and started to show me writings and pictures of these individuals.

I had a complete list of individual names, dates, and migration patterns by the time I was handing in this project. I absolutely was hooked and this little project blossomed into a full blown part-time job that I have done over the course of my life and my parent's lives.

Therefore, you start with the people who are around you now – your siblings, parents, uncles, aunts, grandparents, etc. Sit with them, have conversations with them, be sure to take a recording device and picture taking device. Do not be surprised if you have many different conversations, or little trips you may take together – either to go to a family cemetery, to a church the family used to belong to, or to old family homes. As you start to chronical the life and times of your family, these places will be a part of the history and add much rich information about who you are and the identity of your family.

There are many websites and phone applications that have questions as jumping off places to use in family history research. My best advice is you can use them for inspiration, but, follow your curiosity. Sit for a bit and ponder what it is you want to know about your family, and questions will come to you.

If your family is anything like mine, when we got together for family gatherings and events, stories would be told. Capture those stories, or, at the very least, carry a notepad or note taking device where you can jot down a story line to ask about later.

Family events are full of information if you keep your awareness level to a point where you can realize that these gems are right in front of you!

When my family got together, some stories were shared over and over and over again. They sort of get engrained into the family legend, but I promise you, if someone does NOT write them down, they will be lost after one or two generations are gone. It does not take long for memories to fade or potentially lose those memories forever.

Think about it, we know about certain people in history because someone chose to write things down. Prior to the masses knowing how to read and write, people who thought their lives mattered had personal biographers following them around. Even though today, most everyone can read and write, we have to think of ourselves as those people who felt their lives mattered – and matter enough to have their life story written down for future generations. Why? Because it does matter.

If, for any reason, you think or feel that this sounds arrogant, please challenge that feeling. Without the feeling that your life matters, and those around you matter, future generations that follow you will only know you by a birth date, a death date, perhaps a marriage certificate, a census entry, or a will. While these pieces of information are great – it is better than nothing – it is a pretty sterile view of your life. The goal is to go beyond the stats and get into the heart and soul of your rich family tree – future generations will thank you!

Always, always get permission to include items, especially if the person is still alive. Thus, ask people ahead of time if you can record stories they tell and if it is ok to include them in your collection, and especially get their permission if you publish. I have always given a free book to anyone who contributes to my books!

Summary

1. Start with your immediate, living family

2. Be curious and ask a lot of questions

3. Write the stories down

4. Have a good recorder

5. Have a way of keeping notes and action items

6. Have a good camera

7. Be OPEN to new tools!

Pictures

I am sure you have seen the family member that has a box FULL of pictures. This was my family, too. My parents had a box of photos AND many photo albums. Pictures can be a wealth of family information to be preserved and there are several different ways of doing this important work for your family tree.

Everyone has their own value set, and there is NOTHING wrong with keeping the actual photos. The key is keeping the actual photos in good shape. However, what I like to do is to keep photos in an electronic format. I will explain how I do that.

However, before I describe my process, it is important to sit down with those individuals that know the people in the photos so that you can write down all of the names. There is nothing worse than inheriting some photographs that no one knows who the individual(s) are.

Now that you now who is in the photographs, I follow a process of electronically save the photos. Many photographs that are in boxes have no electronic record, because they were taken with camera with film that had to be processed. Today, we have the advantage of having cameras that automatically create electronic copies.

When you are faced with that big box of photos, take your digital camera, or you handy dandy smart phone and start taking picture of the pictures. Make sure the phot can lie flat and make sure you have good lighting, however be very aware if the light is shining off the photograph. If you take the picture, and see a shine from the lighting, make adjustments can take it again so that you get a clear photograph of the original photograph. In addition, make sure the photo is as "square" in your shot as possible.

For example, check out this picture of a death certificate:

Once we crop this photograph, we can actually just have the details in the center all completely captured, without any of the table or surface that the picture was taken on, plus, the picture will not be tilted.

Here is how the photo looks once it is

cropped with Snag It © software

http://bit.ly/tech-smith:

Contrast this photo to the following:

See how the photo is not centered? If we try to crop this one, we will still get some of the background in the photo that you really do not want to have.

If we try to crop it, the cropping job

will be still capturing some of the surface

behind the photograph:

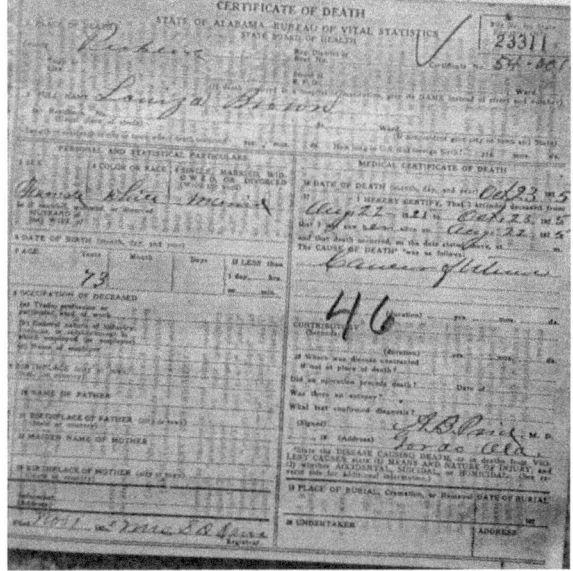

Letters

Over the course of my journey in researching my family tree, the biggest joy I get is finding personal letters or diary entries. This can include, believe it or not, homework that has been saved. So be sure that this is one of the FIRST questions you ask people – do they have any saved letters that they would like to be preserved?

If a person says they do have letters and would like for them to be preserved, they may not be willing to allow you to take them from their possession in order for you to copy them. Some individuals may have a copier in their home, but at the very least, this is why you always want to carry a camera device of some sort with you when you visit with family members.

What I like to do, especially if the letter is hand written, is to take a picture of the letter, or a page of the letter. The reason to do this is because paper is something that is difficult to save over the ravages of time. This also gives future generations a chance to see the handwriting of the individual, something that can definitely get lost quickly if we are not careful.

A few other things to consider around letters. First, you may want to protect the papers by having them laminated, or something like that, in order to have these preserved for a long time to come. However, you will need to type the letters up, and this can be a challenge in reading other people's writing, but it can be done. You may need to get a magnifying glass, just because it will make the letters a little bigger so that you can see patterns in how people write. Sometimes, though, a word might not be legible. In that case, just indicates that words or phrases were not legible.

You may find that people have information that is already typed up, or they may have marriage certificates, enlistment papers, and various other documents that you would want to preserve. Try not to get into the mindset of deciding at the time if you want to preserve something, take the gifts as they arrive! I have found that for the most part, I preserve most anything gifted to me in terms of borrowing or taking over ownership of the family treasure.

Courthouse

The courthouse is a great place to go explore your family tree. When you establish where your family has migrated in terms of geography, the courthouse can become a great place to find the statistical data – things like property deeds, marriages licenses, copies of wills, or divorce papers.

So many people have researched their family that staff in courthouses are very helpful in showing you the ropes of looking up information and being able to copy records.

Be aware, too, that the courthouse buildings may have a section where they keep all of the previous editions of newspapers. This can be a wealth of information, too, just know that you will possibly be spending hours looking through them, so you want to have years that you want to search.

For example, in Pickens County, Alabama, my mother and I went to the courthouse to look through the newspaper archives. I had learned that my grandfather had been a really good quarterback for the local high school in 1935-1936. In addition, my father had been on a winning football team in 1954-1955. We were curious if we would find any mention of them in the paper. We scoured those years in the archives, but football was not covered in those years like it is today, so we did not find anything. We did not let that discourage us, though, because even though we did not find what we were looking for, we found many other articles and then we were inspired to look through other years. The reason we likely found anything at all is because all fours branches on my family tree has lived in Pickens County, Alabama for around 150 years.

Be prepared though, if you are looking through newspaper archives, often there is no index. Thus, you will be looking through page by page of a newspaper so plan accordingly with your time!

Going to the courthouse can be very fruitful. For instance, a recent experience of mine is quite interesting. I knew that one of my two times great grandmothers had gotten a divorce back in 1902. On ancestry.com it is possible to find the entry that the divorce occurred (however, in this case, I could not find it on the electronic databases), but I knew that this record existed. Why? Because I had been at the courthouse one day going through files and ran across it – I knew to look for it because a family member had a vague recollection that this event had occurred. I hunted for it and found it very easily. Therefore, the courthouse can still be a great place to find details of events. In a divorce, witnesses come forward with affidavits to support the parties involved, and believe me, this one is a hoot to read!

In addition, I knew that my maternal grandfather was the subject (along with his siblings) in a custody battle after his mother died when he was ten years old. Everyone knew it, but I could only find the actual document at the courthouse – at this time, ancestry.com does not have those kinds of documents that I can see.

Basically, even with technology being what it is today, sometimes you are going to have to spend the time and effort to actually drive to a courthouse, near or far, to find some of the gems of your family history. This is not a bad thing – you will find that some of these types of records and details can be very enlightening on giving you a glimpse into an ancestor's life and times.

Library

The library can be a great place to go research your family tree. While you will not find the typical courthouse records, what you may discover is a book where someone else has researched someone in your family tree.

When I was first starting out on my family research journey, I knew that my family has migrated through Georgia. After college, I found myself living in the Atlanta, GA area and one of my treks I took was to go to the State Archives building location in Atlanta to see what I could find.

As I was searching through the card catalogue, I was looking for surnames in my family tree, and lo and behold, I discover a book by an author that we shared the surname of Bonner and the title of his book was about migration patterns of the Bonner family.

I went to pull the book off the shelf and I was blown away. Someone before me had done a tremendous amount of research on the Bonner family and had a ton of information about the family in Georgia. I found out many fascinating pieces of information including the fact that I found the Revolutionary War connection for the Bonner family and I found out that one of the descendants was a very wealthy man who owned a gold mine in Georgia. This one book was an important resource for me to be able to fill in several generations of my family prior to their migration to Alabama in the early 1800s.

The other thing you can find are microfilm and microfiche of census records. This may be becoming less of a hassle these days, because with the advent of the websites like ancestry.com a lot of the records have been converted to electronic databases online and the technology is a lot smarter to find possible family matches. If you find yourself going through microfiche or microfilm for any reason, it is not an indexed resource, so your eyes might get fuzzy rolling through page after page looking for family surnames. Be prepared

that you may only get through one or two

rolls before your eyes just cannot take it

anymore!

Graveyards

Graveyards are places you used to have to trek to, yet today we can find out a lot about graveyard information through electronic means. However, that does not get away from the fact that sometimes it feels like a pilgrimage to find grave sites of family members.

Remember, a lot of graveyards are getting lost to time. Some graveyards were in areas where the churches perhaps are gone and the graveyard has grown over. Be prepared with hiking clothing and shoes that can keep you from getting scratched up or will ruin your clothes and shoes.

This may require going to an area and starting to talk to people who may know about the graveyard. For example, on one of my visits with my mother, she told me she had found the grave of my two times great grandmother. See, my mother's mother knew where the graveyard was located. Mom showed me the road where she is buried, but we thought we would have time to go again. Sadly, she passed before we could go again.

I know that when I go back there, I will have to be knocking on doors and asking people if they know where this graveyard is because it is in the woods. The reason I want to go there, because hey, my mom had already gone there is this: I want to mark the place with a GPS coordinate. It is one thing to get a picture of the grave stone, but it is another thing entirely to get the coordinates of where the grave is located. In the future, when many generations have past, a road or other landmark is not present, being able to find a location will be important. This is important, because landmarks decay, are moved, are changed – and in the future you may want to find things. I will discuss this more in the GPS tools section in the technology chapter.

Reflection

Even with the technology tools we have today, using the method of actually driving or hiking to a source can still have rewarding results for you as a family researcher and historian. The nice thing is there are lots of helpful individuals out there that can help you look for things – take advantage of them. They are the most knowledgeable about the systems used to archive data in their courthouse and they can be very useful in helping you find information. Use everything at your disposal to maximize your time and effort. Plus, sometimes these can make great vacations – especially if you have to drive longer than a few hours to a particular courthouse. My parents, when they were in their retirement, used their RV to go all over the country and they researched the family history all at the same time. Sometimes they struck gold, sometimes it was a bust, but they had a good time!

CHAPTER 2: TECHNOLOGY TOOLS

Once you gather all of your data, you will need a place to store your information. Everyone has their own preferences, for example, I am well aware that some people are very kinesthetic – in other words, they like to touch and feel their collection. If you are that type of person, you may actually keep a lot more paper than someone else, just be aware that paper is something that will need careful attention to be preserved.

For instance, I had found out that my uncle had copies of love letters between my paternal grandmother and grandfather while he was stationed in Japan during WWII. These letters, once I learned about them, were a bit moldy and were not good around people with asthma. Thus, I chose NOT to obtain the originals, he was perfectly willing to give them to me, but he also had copies of the letters.

I thought it would be best for my family for me not to have letters that would trigger asthma in my family members, so I decided the copies would be fine and processed them and personally archived them from there.

If you are a person that is not kinesthetic, an electronic copy will likely suffice. For me, I find this to be the easiest way for me to keep track of items. Not everything I have can be saved electronically. For example, I have a dress sword from WWII that belonged to my paternal grandfather. There is no other way to preserve that than to keep it and eventually find the individual that wants to keep it after my passing. I can document it, take a picture of it, and make sure it is in my will.

Ultimately, the idea is to have a strategy of how you will keep track of all the information. Think about this, I have over 1,000 electronic pictures catalogued, and I have several diaries, letters, reminisces and other items transcribed. Believe me, I have sat at a computer for several hours and one of the big concerns is how to ensure the longevity of these materials for future generations.

For one thing, if you keep physical artifacts, you have to worry about fire or water damage destroying the items and this is one of the reasons I like keeping electronic copies where I can. The vast majority of what I have preserved is electronic now.

Of course, a file can get corrupted, or you can some way or another lose an electronic file, but there are ways to minimize that risk. One way is to have a backup of your system done periodically and there are various companies like Carbonite that can do this for a yearly maintenance fee or you can have a backup system that encompasses a separate hard drive on your computer or backing up files to a CD. Plus, ancestry.com allows you to keep various files on its servers on an electronic depiction of your family tree.

The idea here is that you have to have a plan, especially when you start having so many artifacts that you are managing as your family historian. A high degree of organizational skill comes in handy for a family historian, and if that is not your skill, find a family member that is organized to help you – you will find this to be a very valuable collaboration!

Finally, you may have to make provisions in your last will and testament about the disbursement of these artifacts. This could be as simple as providing a list of items and who in your family should receive them, but this may also involve more of a formal document about how to handle the entirety of your collection. For example, in my case, I will have to have a document that outlines what to do with the transfer of the books that I have written, the income streams for those books, all of the backup information as well as all of the artifacts and if I would like them donated to a museum. Do your legwork so your work is not in vain!

Ancestry.com

One of the best tools to come along has been ancestry.com. The biggest boon this website has brought to the family researcher is the ability to cut down on a lot of driving and hors of sitting in front of non-indexed resources.

For example, if you remember, I talked about having to read through newspapers page by page, or having to look through microfilm of a census report. On ancestry, there are many databases that exist in the system and many more get added every year. In fact, most recently, the 1940 census database has been added. This was the first time that I saw my father on a census pop up as a "hint" on ancestry. This allows you to enter information about a family member, i.e., name, birthdate, and other identifying information and the search engine will bring back to you these hints that are suggesting records that might be your ancestor. The engine is pretty smart and it looks for derivations of the name and dates that are exact or in close proximity, it is then your job to evaluate the relevance of these little pieces of information.

Another really cool thing about ancestry.com is it allows you to keep recordings and video. For instance, when I recorded stories at my parent's memorials, I could save them there. Plus, I have recording of performances where I have played drums and have placed recordings on the profile of myself on ancestry. In addition, after my paternal grandparents died, my mother found an old cassette of them singing Baptist hymns together. I found a cassette recorder that allows me to record off of the cassette, onto my computer, and the output becomes an .mp3 file. I have gotten several recordings onto my computer using that method and then I can save them for posterity.

When my mother died, a friend of the family had recorded some video of her on their phone. She posted the video to Facebook and I went to Google to find how to download those video files. There is a great tutorial out there on how to do it, and then I can save them in my collections as well.

The real key to all of this is to not be intimidated by the technology and you will soon realize Google becomes your best friend on how to handle the challenges you might face in keeping good copies.

For instance, the cassette recordings of my paternal grandparents needed some work. Therefore, I had to learn how to do some editing of the files. This is when I got a subscription to Adobe and re-mastered the .mp3 files so that they had a bit more volume and some of the "hissiness" was taken out. I knew I had done this well when one of the nephews of my paternal grandparents cried over the recordings – he had not heard their voices together in over twenty years at the point he heard them in my recordings I sent to him.

Google Earth

Google Earth is a free tool and what is so great about it is that you can mark places where you have lived, worked, vacationed, etc. This is a tool that I have used to tell stories about my family. For instance, the Bonner women, back in the American Revolution, were involved in a political action against Great Britain. Thus, I was able to highlight the town of Edenton, North Carolina, where this took place, and take a picture of it and used it in a video where I told the story about this event in American History.

There are many uses for this tool in showing how a family has migrated over time and it will give future generations the coordinates for GPS positioning for where you childhood home used to be (even if over time the house no longer exists).

Finally, another really cool feature is that you can go down to the "street" level in some areas, especially in cities, and get pictures of homes, buildings, etc., without having to travel to the location to get a picture of your own. For instance, my great grandfather owned a home in Birmingham, Alabama, and I had an old photograph of the house. I was curious one day and looked it up n Google Earth and was able to take a picture of it as recently as 2014. Or, let's say that I did not have a picture of the house, since I have the address, I could get a picture of it, if the house still exists.

You never know, out of all of the information you know about your family, you are likely to find a great many treasures on Google Earth and be able to tell the story of your family in truly unique ways.

Camtasia (Video Editing)

At some point, I had so many photographs of my family, it just seemed like printing them all in a book did not make sense. At that time, I was also learning how to build a YouTube channel, so I thought it might be really cool to supplement my family history books with YouTube content.

This way, I could include all kinds of family photos, as I told stories about my family in video format. As I have told stories about my parents, or my grandparents, I was able to use so many photographs that I have saved over time.

Camtasia (http://bit.ly/tech-smith) is the Windows platform software that I use – I have found it to be the most flexible and has really great features to take advantage of in creating great videos.

Now, there is a lot of detail in learning how to make really nice videos, and on my YouTube channel (http://tiny.cc/KTDA), you can subscribe to be sure that you are alerted about new, free video content that will go through how to develop a video about your cool family stories.

The other thing to remember, is if you do obtain a video camera, or even if you are using your smartphone, you want to have good audio quality. One thing I recommend is having Movavi Suite – download here (http://bit.ly/movavi1) – this has great tools, not only for converting video footage (i.e., from a video camera), but you also have the ability to create wonderful voice quality on the voice track in a video. On the YouTube Channel, I will provide details on how all of these tools work together, with a focus on keeping your costs minimal.

Smart Phone Applications

Smart phones have become great tools for the family researcher. In fact, you no longer have to have a separate camera to haul around, I have used my phone camera to capture many photographs for my family history.

Ancestry.com has its own applications that can be downloaded. Check their website for the latest, or check the online store for your phone device. For example they have a "Find a Grave" application and a "Shoebox" application available. One great thing about Ancestry is you can actually download your tree(s) to your phone so that you can see them while out and about, so if you need to check a date or something while at a courthouse, or library, or with a distant cousin you have just located, all the information is at our fingertips in an easy application.

GPS applications are a great thing to use. In March 2014, when visiting my mother, we decided to stop by the home place of my paternal grandparents. The house still exists, however, the lot where their house stands is starting to grow over. One of the huge trees in the yard had fallen over. I realized that before too long, future generations may not be able to find this house. Just down below the hill, one of his sister's houses is already gone. I decided to take a photo, but I decided also to use the compass on my phone to capture the coordinates.

Based on doing this one location that way, my mother and I spent most of the day going to all of the places she and my father had lived, we had lived, and I took pictures along with the compass GPS coordinates so that future generations would have a chance of being able to find the location.

The more accurate GPS locations you can get are from the Google Earth (http://www.google.com/earth/download/ge/agree.html) application. I have found this one application to be the best for marking locations on a map so that I can preserve them forever.

Voice Recorder/Audio Converter and Editing – The great thing about our smartphones today is that they are already taking excellent video. So, if you go to a reunion, take your smartphone. But you will need a good microphone if you want better audio quality. Now, I have some audio of my parents, using the smartphone, and it is ok, and frankly it is better than nothing!

However, if you want to have good audio without having to edit it once you get home then purchase yourself a fairly inexpensive lavalier microphone (http://bit.ly/lavalier-as). They plug right into your phone and then that microphone is the audio that gets recorded through whichever voice recorder you download to your phone. The voice recorder I use is called Easy Voice Recorder Pro – just look for something that allows you to upload the audio files to Dropbox or Google Drive or One Drive.

Now, if you do have the need for editing the sound quality, use Audacity (http://audacityteam.org/). It is a free tool. When my mother found a cassette of my grandparents singing together, the audio quality was pretty bad. However, I was able to get that audio off of the cassette, into an .mp3 file, and was able to make the quality of it sound pretty good using Audacity. You can find the cassette to .mp3 converters on Amazon – like this one here (http://bit.ly/converter-as).

Snag It! Software

When I tried publishing a family history book for the first time, I ran into issues with the photographs. The publishing platform I use is one that requires a certain number of Dots per Inch (DPI) on the photos so that they look good once published.

I researched how to fix this and the Snag It! Software © came up as a solution (purchase and download here: http://bit.ly/tech-smith). I have found it to be an extremely reliable piece of software for a minimal investment. Just google Snag It software and the website will pop up for Techsmith where you can purchase it.

When I take a picture with my phone, the usual dots per inch is 144. When I open the picture in Snag It, I go to "Image", "Resize", and then click on "Resize Image. In a little box there is a "Resolution" and next to it and then change the number in the box if it is not 300, as seen in the picture below:

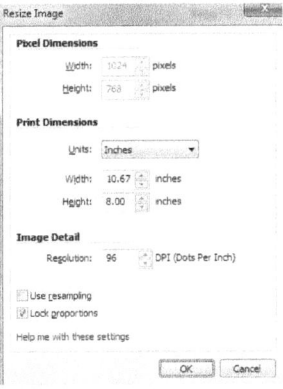

Re-save the file so that the resolution is now changed. Now you can insert the picture into your document and the right

DPI will be there for the book to be printed

and not cause an error on your upload of the

Microsoft Word document of your

manuscript. I use Snag it for so many other

things that the small investment makes it

worth it to me, editing pictures is just one of

the benefits.

Online Storage

A downside of keeping files on a hard drive is that we used to not be able to take out computers with us. With the advent of personal computing, all of that has changed. Nowadays, you can take a laptop with you. But, more importantly, you do not necessarily have to do that anymore!

I have used storage on Dropbox, Google docs, and One Drive. I tend to prefer, these days, either Google docs or One Drive because they allow more free capacity.

Why would you want to keep your documents and files on one of these? One good example is that smart phone apps can upload to these websites directly. This can be very useful and I will give you an example.

As I sat in a little country church in Coalfire, Alabama in May 2014 for my father's memorial service, I had an epiphany. My mother had wanted to have a celebration of his life, instead of the typical funeral. She wanted everyone to have the opportunity if they wanted to share stories about my dad. I wanted to capture these because I was sure I had never heard some of this before!

I quickly found an application that would record and upload audio to Dropbox. I sat in the congregation and recorded the stories and believe me, they were quite humorous. Then, because they uploaded to Dropbox, I did not have to do anything else with the files. I did not have to transcribe them. I did not have to try and get them recorded off of my phone.

Another great benefit to having the storage websites is that you can access these files anywhere. Thus, if you do not, for some reason, have your laptop with you, you can logon any computer and get to your files.

In addition, for full flexibility, I can also access these files through my smart phone to the smart phone applications they have. You may not want to do full fledge editing on a file in a smart phone – that would be too tedious, but if you wanted to check something or access the files on the fly – you could. This comes in handy with the pictures. Especially if you are in front of someone that may have information on a photo and you want to show it to them to jog their memory.

Reflection

There will be many tools you will use in your family research journey. New tools will pop up over time, and this book only gives you a flavor for what I have used. The goal is to help you be comfortable in what I use and to increase your comfort level in trying different tools. In the age of technology, this will likely not be a problem and you can be grateful that you are no longer having to try and type up a manuscript on a typewriter or try to work around film loaded cameras. Technology has truly paved the way for you to be a writer and to publish in a relatively cheap, but still professional, manner.

CHAPTER 3: WRITING A BOOK

Writing a family history book is sometimes the ultimate goal of doing family research. Many people never do this and there could be a number of reasons a person may decide not to do this important step.

For one, in the past to publish a book required quite a bit of money to be fronted to the publisher. For example, when my parents first published their books in the 1990s, my parents had to PAY the publishing company to print a certain number of books. By printing in volume like that, the publishing company could keep the costs down and thus my parents were able to keep the costs down to the people who might want to purchase their books.

However, when my dad published the first Bonner Family History, it was a two volume set, well over 1,000 pages, and he sold it for $75. It was quite the investment for them to do this, and over several years they slowly but surely sold just about every book. Ultimately, they were able to recoup their cost plus a little bit more.

Now, there are much cheaper alternatives for publishing. However, keep in mind that publishing is a separate thing to writing the actual contents of the book. The way I will describe for you to publish takes the guesswork out of the publishing part, and trust me, for many people, the idea of writing a book is daunting. Remember when I said that a person needs to have good organization skills? You have to be organized as a writer, too, and the biggest challenge with writing a book is how to organize the contents.

However, I am going to show you a template: download here (http://tiny.cc/fhbtemplate) that I use for writing my family history books and they are a great place to start. Over time, you may find that something clsc works for you, and that is fine, but if you have no clue, at least this can get you started. In fact, I am happy to share my Word template in its entirety – download here:

http://tiny.cc/fhbtemplate. In addition to the template, I am building free video content to explain how to use the template – please visit the Keep the Dash Alive YouTube Channel (http://tiny.cc/KTDA) and be sure to subscribe – that way you will be notified when new video content is uploaded.

Organizing the Book

My parents first published the family history books through a publisher in the 1990s. At that time, as a write of family history books, you had to front the money for a large volume purchase. For example, my parents gave me a rough estimate that they had to pay $5,000 upfront, let's say for

100 books. They would do this in order to keep costs down – if they were to buy books as orders came in, the individual books may have cost $120 and likely there would be few sales.

A few other downsides existed. For instance, my parents had to have a place to store these books so that they did not get ruined. Thus keeping the books away from water damage or stains was a big concern. In addition, family history books should contain a certain amount of photos because this is one of those things that brings family history to life. However, to reduce costs of production, the books had to have all of the photos within one section or chapter. If they had wanted a photo to be on the page where a person was mentioned in the book, the publisher had to overlay that page with a picture page – thus increasing the costs.

Upon visiting with my mother in March, 2014, we got onto the subject of family history as we always did. It dawned on me in this conversation that I had already published one book through Amazon and Createspace, and I could get the family history books on the platforms as well so that she would not have to keep any inventory of books on hand. Plus, we were talking about the fact that she was practically out of books, and she did not want to spend the investment anymore to have to buy another round of inventory. She

was completely on board and was excited to

have them recreated on these platforms.

I ended up having to recreate them from scratch. This allowed me to make some organizational revisions to the books a well. One of the most ponderous parts of writing a family history book is keeping track of where you are in the tree. In fact, in reproducing my father's Bonner History Book – this book is a two volume set and it goes into excruciating detail on various lines of the family tree. Trying to keep track of where I was in the tree was a daunting task.

As I pondered how to handle this, I decided that I was going to organize the book by generation. Thus, on the Bonner side of my family, I can go back thirteen generations with certainty. Plus, as new generations are born, they can be added in, no problem, as a new chapter heading.

Now what do I mean by chapter heading? In Microsoft Word, you have the ability to insert a "Table of Contents" under the "References" tab of the menu ribbon. The table of contents is driven off of "Styles" in the software. Thus, I build a Table of Contents where the "Heading 1" style was my higher level grouping. This, any "Heading 1" became "Generation 1", "Generation 2", "Generation 3" and so one.

Within the table of contents, I also used "Heading 2" – and this became individual names, like "Henry Bonner", or

"Woodrow Cecil Bonner". What is nice about this process is the table of contents then gives you a hyperlink where you can go to a section of your book quickly without having to page through the document.

In addition to this, you can also go one heading level deeper to "Heading 3". I used this at times when I had several other artifacts for a specific person. For instance, with Woodrow Cecil Bonner, I had a reflection that my father had written about him, I had his obituary, and I had a reflection written by my grandmother about him. All of these can have the "Heading 3" style applied to the header of the artifact and this will be captured in the Table of

Contents so a reader can get to the artifacts quickly.

Currently, in Microsoft Word, you add a Table of Contents in the "References" Tab of the ribbon in Microsoft Word 2013 version. If this ever changes, just do a search in the help function of Microsoft and search on the term, "Table of Contents" and the system will give you instructions on the exact menu path to follow in future versions of the software (just in case it gets moved).

If you would like a copy of my family history book template, download here: http://tiny.cc/fhbtemplate. In addition to the template, I am building free video content to explain how to use the template –

please visit the Keep the Dash Alive

YouTube Channel (http://tiny.cc/KTDA)

and be sure to subscribe – that way you will

be notified when new video content is

uploaded.

Table of Figures

I use the "Insert Table of Figures" to create an index of the pictures. The nice thing about this feature is that I can have pictures throughout the book, on any page I desire, and the entire collection of pictures is then in a table list along with the page number of where to find the picture.

For my "Table of Figures" I changed the name of it to "List of Pictures" and it comes right after the Table of Contents in my book. If you would like a copy of my family history book template, download here: http://tiny.cc/fhbtemplate. In addition to the template, I am building free video content to explain how to use the template –

please visit the Keep the Dash Alive

YouTube Channel (http://tiny.cc/KTDA)

and be sure to subscribe – that way you will

be notified when new video content is

uploaded.

Index of Names

In addition, I use the "Insert Index" function in Microsoft Word to create my Index of names at the end of the book. Then, in order to automatically "fill" the Index of names, you have to "Mark Entry" on names within the body of the book.

For example, many of my chapter headings are a person's name, with parentheses that hold the birth year and death year. Here is an example:

GENERATION 1
Anthony Bonner III (1564 – 1650)

The type of this header does not automatically insert Anthony Bonner III into my Index of Names, I actually have to mark the entry so that Microsoft Word knows to insert it. Therefore, I need to highlight his name with the cursor, go to the "References" tab in Word, and click "Mark Entry". When I do this, I get an interactive box for me to type in as seen below:

Since I want my names to be listed alphabetically by last name, I need to make an adjustment to the above entry. Plus, if I have a birth year, I include it with the name.

Thus, my marked entry would be this:

This takes quite a bit of detail oriented work to ensure that you have all names indexed in your book, but it is well worth the time. Just do not forget, when you add new people, they need to be indexed as well.

Plus, and this is REALLY important, if you copy and paste sections of your book. The index may not actually match up to the name. For example, if I copied "Anthony

Bonner's" section to a new section (so I do not have to type the framework over and over of the detail on the person, then I need to remember the index goes with it. Thus, if this new section is about "Henry Bonner", then I need to make sure the index entry on it is changed, too.

Publishing

In 2013, I decided it was a lifelong goal of mine to publish a book. It was equally important, for me, that I not worry too much about the books contents, because my big learning curve was going to be on the actual publishing process. I had written a lot during my school work through my doctorate, plus, I teach and have to critique writing. So, to focus on the publishing process, I decided to write a memoir so that the book writing was not an issue (I should at least not have to research my life).

I started asking around with people that had writing experience, trying to find out if they had published or not, what publishing route they had taken, etc. I quickly found out that many people have gone the traditional publishing route and when I told them I was writing a biography for my first book, every single person told me it would not sell – because you are not famous! Well, I actually did not care at the time if the book sold or not, I just wanted to learn how to publish and felt that would be the easiest thing to write.

I kept the idea in the back of my mind and eventually ran into someone I was working with at the time that was writing her own book for the first time. Around the same time I met her, I had learned about Createspace.com. I was not quite sure about it being the platform I wanted to use, but it looked promising. As it turned out, my co-worker was looking at the same site and we determined it was the best place to get published.

From that point on, there was no looking back. Now, you can spend lots of money to have createspace employee's help you do book covers and various other services they can provide, however, you can get by very cheaply on the site for publishing. I can do much of my own editing and I can publish a book for as little as ZERO dollars. All it really costs is my time.

In some cases you may have a desire to do more by adding a cool book cover rather than the free templates they have – for instance, I have taken my own pictures for book covers (i.e., like a really cool tree, for a family history book). Eventually I may do more with the site, but for now, I use it to get published.

Another cool feature of the createspace website is that once you have published your softcover book there, you have the option to move the book over to Kindle Direct Publishing (KDP) to create a Kindle formatted book on Amazon. The great thing is that you can get the softcover book AND the kindle book on Amazon so that whatever the reader prefers, they can

purchase the format that they like.

Reflection

Writing a book about your family history is a huge accomplishment and one that I encourage people to undertake. It is a very satisfying experience, because there will be people interested in the topic and you will see people be very moved by being able to see pictures and memorabilia in printed format.

The biggest hurdles are gathering the information, but more importantly, organizing it so that people can follow along with the generations. If my template can help you, download it here http://tiny.cc/fhbtemplate. In addition to the template, I am building free video content to explain how to use the template – please visit the Keep the Dash Alive YouTube Channel (http://tiny.cc/KTDA) and be sure to subscribe – that way you will be notified when new video content is uploaded.

CHAPTER 4: MARKETING

No matter what, you will have to some degree market your book. Now, what is nice is that you can certainly sell a lot of books at family functions and when people find out you have a book, they will come knocking on your door. However, there is only so many of those books you can sell, so you want to create visibility to your family history books in other ways.

Getting awareness out there for a family history book is a little bit different in some respects, but you have to employ one skill – creativity. Finding ways to get more people to know of your book is one of the fun adventures of the entire process.

KINDLE

One of the nice things about the Kindle format is that Kindle users can let friends borrow their copy of the book – and this is a good thing because you still get paid for the book when the book is borrowed. Amazon has a Kindle Library Lending fund they have created to pay out a percentage of the fund when the book is borrowed.

Secondly, the Kindle format allows you to set up a free giveaway of your book. The free giveaway you can do a few times a year and I have found this to increase awareness of my books. Remember when I told you that my first foray into learning about publishing writers told me my autobiography would not sell? Well, through various methods I have employed, my book has sold 229 copies as of the time I have published this book. Now, since my goal was not necessarily to have gangbuster sales, and because I was just using it to learn, the sales of course have exceeded my expectations. Out of those sales, most of the sales are from free giveaways, however, the book has been borrowed quite a bit, which pays me, too.

The nice thing, too about Createpsace and KDP is that you can sell your books globally. On KDP, for my autobiography book, out of the 229 book sales, I have sold them around the world –

here is a breakdown (which does include

borrowed units):

United States	171
Great Britain	29
Germany	9
Canada	6
India	2
Australia	1
Italy	1
Japan	1
Spain	1

The goal for me in writing the

history books on the other hand, of course, I

would like to make my money back as far as

my time and effort in getting them

published, and the more I can increase the

awareness that the books exist, then my future generations, too, will have a legacy where they can take over the publishing of the books and perhaps have a stream of income.

One way of getting awareness out there is through sending your history books to libraries as gifts. This is even easier than before because in the past, when my parents published the books the first time, they bought the books outright and they gifted the books to the libraries near them. Now, of course they paid a lot more for the book than I can.

On Createspace, if I have a book that is 200 pages long, the cost of actually printing the book is less than $10. Let that sink in. Where my parents HAD to buy their books for $75 each, I do NOT have to buy ANY books, and I can buy them AT COST (less than $10) and send them to libraries all over the country. If a relative goes into a library and looks for family surnames, they could find my book, they might like it and want to have a copy of their own, and I state in the book that they can have their own copy through Amazon.

QR Codes

There is a great website called qrstuff.com. A QR Code looks like this:

These codes are something that smart phones can read. For example, I could create a QR Code that links directly to my family history book on Amazon. Thus, if someone scans the code, it takes them directly to the book, or Kindle book, to purchase it.

These codes can be printed on business cards, mugs, pens, notebooks, t-shirts, etc. The QR code is free, but the business cards, or other items you can have them printed on, are not free. So be aware of that!

I have used the QR codes on business cards very nicely – buying 500 business cards on VistaPrint.com is not too expensive and I can have those ready to hand out anytime and it would take a while to go through 500 of them.

Gifts to Libraries

One great way to get visibility to your book is to send gift copies to libraries and archives. You can sit down with Google search and look up libraries in cities and archives in different states. Start making a list of the address, phone number, and emails of the libraries and if possible the librarian name may be listed as well.

Find out who the librarian is, regardless, if this means calling them and explain that you would like to gift books to their library about your family history. I have yet to have any library or archive turn me down.

Even better, on createspace, you can order the book for the cost of the book, not the retail price. If the retail price is $19.99, or $29.99, your actually printing cost may be less than $5. Therefore, you can ship a copy to a library at cost plus shipping. This way, anyone going to research their family history has an opportunity to run into your book.

Not very many family history books are on Amazon right now as of the time of publication of this book, thus people are not looking there. However, if they find your book in a library or an archive, you can mention in your book that the book is available on Amazon as a soft cover book and a Kindle book, whichever they prefer to obtain.

Finally, over time you can get books into many libraries – your local libraries, even if your family did not reside there is still a great place for family history books. I grew up in Pickens County, Alabama, and many generations my family lines lived there over many decades. When I moved away, I moved to places where not a whole lot of close family members live, but, you never know who might be searching for the information you have compiled. From a priority perspective though, hit the places you know family has migrated to, those will likely be your big hitter libraries for

awareness of your research.

Reflection

Marketing beyond our immediate family is not something that family researchers may think much about. Plus, if your goal is to create a format for your immediate family, then you may not actually think much further. However, if you want your book to reach people you may never have thought of, then some of the marketing ideas in this book may help you to find avenues for your book to be seen around the world.

CHAPTER 5: ONGOING RESEARCH

One of the traps your brain can get you with is thinking you have to have it all researched before publishing. However, your family research is something that will likely be ongoing. You may find new letters, or a new diary, or a whole bunch of new photos.

This does not mean that you need to create an update to your book, but you want to be ready to do so, if you would like to. When my mother also passed in 2014, only about four months after my father, as we cleaned out her apartment, I found many items that I wanted to save and preserve for the future. This included pictures and mementos that I thought would be a great addition to the family history books. I found so many photographs and certificates that I thought maybe I would want to do a Bonner Family scrapbook and photo album combination.

The point is, you decide if you want to create a new version of your book. You can have your own criteria for when and why you would want to do this. One thing is for sure, as new generations are born, new versions can be done going forward. You may or may not find information going backward to add to your collection, but it is possible!

LIST OF RESOURCES

Ancestry: www.ancestry.com

Snag It Software: http://bit.ly/tech-smith

Camtasia Software: http://bit.ly/tech-smith

Createspace.com: www.createspace.com

Kindle Direct Publishing (KDP):

kdp.amazon.com

Qrstuff: www.qrstuff.com

Vistaprint: www.vistaprint.com

Dropbox: www.dropbox.com

OneDrive: onedrive.live.com

Google Drive: drive.google.com

Movavi Video Suite: http://bit.ly/movavi1

You Tube Channel http://tiny.cc/KTDA

ABOUT THE AUTHOR

Dr. Julie Bonner is a coach, speaker, consultant, teacher and author living in Redmond, WA. Dr. Bonner teaches full-time as an assistant professor at Central Washington University in Ellensburg, WA.

Dr. Bonner is an author dedicated to providing her readers with very practical information they can use right now on various topics. Dr. Bonner can be contacted by email at KeeptheDashAlive@gmail.com and her Amazon author page is located at http://www.amazon.com/-/e/B00FOBQ4ZK.